SIPPS

SET 2

Toy Deer

of the Florida Keys

by
Dorothy Francis

Perfection Learning®

Photographs courtesy of Bill Keogh: cover, pp. 5, 6, 11, 12, 13, 14, 19, 21, 22, 23, 24, 26, 29, 30, 32, 33, 35, 39, 40, 43, 45, 49, 50, 53.
Some images copyright www.arttoday.com
Book Design: Randy Messer

Dedication

To Dee, who insisted that I write about the Key deer.

About the Author

Dorothy Francis has written many books and stories for children and adults. She and her husband, Richard, divide their time between Marshalltown, Iowa, and Big Pine Key, Florida.

Ms. Francis holds a bachelor of music degree from the University of Kansas. She has traveled with an all-girl dance band, taught music in public and private schools, and served as a correspondence teacher for the Institute of Children's Literature in Connecticut.

As an environmentalist, her goal is to make her readers aware of the creatures around them and their need for nurture and protection.

PB ISBN-13: 978-0-7891-5033-2
PB ISBN-10: 0-7891-5033-6
RLB ISBN-13: 978-0-7807-9018-6
RLB ISBN-10: 0-7807-9018-9
6 7 8 9 10 11 PP 14 13 12 11 10 09
PPI / 12 / 09

Contents

Chapter 1

Trouble in the Backyard

Tim stood at his bedroom window. Was that a puppy playing under the palm tree? He'd always wanted a pet. And a puppy would be lots of fun.

He looked more closely at the tawny, spotted creature. No, it wasn't a puppy.

He could hardly believe it. But he was looking at a tiny deer.

Tim had just come to the Florida Keys. He was visiting his grandfather. Gramp had told Tim he might see deer.

"Gramp!" Tim called. "Gramp, come quick! There's a baby deer right in your backyard."

Gramp hurried to Tim's room. "Right, Tim. It's a fawn."

"Why, it's so tiny! I could hold it in my hands. Could I keep it as a pet? Please, Gramp. I'd take good care of it. I'm older now. And I'm big enough to care for a pet."

Gramp smiled as they watched the fawn nibble grass. "No, Tim. It's unwise to keep a wild creature as a pet. And it's against the law here on Big Pine Key."

Tim knew Gramp worked at the National Key Deer Refuge. It was a short distance from his house. He had worked there for years.

Gramp knew what was best for the deer. So Tim didn't beg to keep the fawn. He was living with Gramp while his mother recovered from an illness. And he had promised to behave.

"Gramp, look!" Tim grabbed Gramp's arm. "Here comes the Johnsons' collie. It's broken its leash! It's running right toward the fawn!"

Gramp yelled at the collie from the window. Then he ran from the house. He grabbed a broom as he dashed through the kitchen.

"Go home!" Gramp shouted and shook the broom at the collie. "Git! Git!"

When Gramp shouted, the collie ran off. The fawn stood shaking under the palm.

"Look at that cute black marking on its nose," Tim said. "Shouldn't we take Blackie inside to keep him safe?"

"Blackie?" Gramp chuckled. "It's okay to name the fawn, I guess. But take it inside? No. The fawn may seem to be alone. But its mother is probably close by."

Gramp nodded toward the thicket behind their house. "The doe is probably watching us right now. She'll take good care of her baby."

Tim wanted to believe Gramp. But Blackie was so tiny. And that collie was so big! Besides that, there were lots of dogs on Big Pine Key. How would Blackie survive so many dangers?

Chapter

Why So Small?

"Why are the Key deer so small, Gramp?" Tim asked. "Deer grow as big as ponies at home in Iowa."

"Tim, it takes a lot of water to make things grow," answered Gramp.

"Big Pine Key is surrounded by water," Tim pointed out.

"But it's seawater. And the seawater contains salt," Gramp said. "The deer need freshwater. That's why they prefer to live on Big Pine Key.

"Big Pine is different from the other keys. The land is formed of oolite."

Gramp continued. "Oolite is a limestone that's full of sinkholes. Farmers call them 'banana holes.' They sometimes use the holes for growing plants."

"And those banana holes hold rainwater," Tim said. "Right?"

"Right," Gramp said. "The deer live here because there's freshwater to drink. But there's not a lot of it. A shortage of water can hold living things to a small size."

"So that's why the Key deer are like toys," Tim said.

"There are other reasons too," Gramp said. "Many species of plants and animals grow smaller in warm climates."

Gramp continued, "It is always summer in the Florida Keys. So the deer don't need fat to keep them warm."

Gramp's explanation made sense. Big Pine Key was a good spot for miniature deer.

But Blackie was so tiny. How would the fawn learn to find water? Would it find enough to drink during dry months?

"Gramp," Tim said. "Is Blackie a boy deer or a girl deer?"

"That's a good question," Gramp said. "It's too soon to tell just yet. But we'll keep watching the deer. As it grows, we may see horn nubs developing on its head. If that happens, Blackie is a boy—a buck."

"And if that doesn't happen," Tim said. "Then Blackie's a girl."

"That's right," Gramp said. "We'll know Blackie's a doe."

Did Tim want Blackie to be a buck or a doe? He couldn't decide. He just wanted Blackie to be safe from danger.

Chapter

What Happened Years Ago?

"Gramp," Tim said. "How long have these little deer been in the Keys?"

"Nobody knows for sure, Tim," Gramp answered. "The Ice Age happened thousands of years ago. Back then, the Keys were solid land. They weren't islands.

"But the sea rose when the Wisconsin Glacier melted. The rising water covered much of the land. The Keys are the highest points of land. The rest is underwater."

"So animals that couldn't swim were trapped here?" Tim asked.

"Scientists think that's what happened," Gramp replied. "The deer's choice was to make do or die. They chose to make do.

"Historians found the first record of Key deer in a ship's logbook," explained Gramp. "It happened during Columbus's fourth voyage to the New World. A sailor wrote of seeing tiny deer."

"That must have been about 500 years ago," Tim said.

"Right," Gramp agreed. "A Spanish sailor was shipwrecked near here 50 years later. He kept a diary. He wrote that Key West natives used the deer for food."

Tim hated to think of anyone using Blackie for food. No way!

Gramp continued his story. "Another 300 years passed before pioneers settled here. They gave the islands creative names. Little Torch. Big Torch. Summerland. Sugarloaf. Big Pine.

"The islands were hard to tame," Gramp added.

Tim tried to imagine taming an island.

"Mangrove trees surrounded the islands," Gramp said. "Their roots grow several inches above the land and water. Those trees formed a natural barrier."

"What did pioneers find once they

managed to come ashore?" Tim asked.

"They found swarms of mosquitoes," Gramp said. "They found rats. And they found very hot, humid weather."

"Nothing good, huh?"

"Oh, yes." Gramp smiled. "There were good things too. They found wonderful wildlife. White-crowned pigeons. Bald eagles. Great white herons. Giant sea turtles. Raccoons. And the tiny deer. They hunted, killed, and ate many of these creatures."

"Heron stew?" Tim asked. "Turtle burgers? Raccoon soup? Yuck!"

"It's easier to imagine roast venison," Gramp admitted. "But don't blame the pioneers for eating the wildlife. They needed food to live. And at first, there seemed to be an unlimited supply of game. But soon, wildlife became extinct."

"What did the pioneers do then?"

"They had food shipped from the mainland." Gramp touched Tim's arm and pointed. "Look! Look over there in the thicket. Let's go upstairs for a better view."

Tim followed Gramp. What were they about to see?

Chapter 4

Family Reunion

A thicket of trees and grass grew behind Gramp's house. Tim and Gramp reached an upstairs window. Tim looked through leaves and branches.

"Gramp! I see lots of deer. One, two, three . . ." Tim counted to eight. "Why are they all together?"

"They are a family, Tim. In the springtime of her second year, a doe finds a secret place for her fawn to be born.

"The fawn is born with teeth. But for four months, it nurses at its mother's side. For six weeks, the doe and fawn spend time together. The other deer leave them alone in their secret place."

Gramp continued, "The doe leaves the fawn alone much of the time. But she hasn't left it. She does this to protect it.

"A fawn is hard to see. Its protective coloring blends into the thicket. But a doe and a fawn together are easier to see. That's why the doe keeps her distance from her fawn."

"But what if a dog comes near?" Tim looked around for the collie they had seen earlier.

"The doe has ways of warning her fawn of danger," Gramp assured Tim. "She may raise her white flag of a tail as a warning. This gives the fawn two choices. It can drop to the ground motionless. Or it can run for cover."

"What if the fawn doesn't see the white tail?" Tim asked.

"Sometimes the doe will drum the ground with her forefoot," Gramp answered. "That signal tells the fawn to head for cover. But these deer we see now are a family."

Tim stood on tiptoe for a better view.

"Each doe usually travels with a special band of does and fawns," continued Gramp. "These bands are formed for a lifetime. An older doe heads the group. The family includes her offspring and all of their offspring."

"So we're watching a family reunion," Tim said.

"A reunion that lasts all summer," Gramp said. "It's a time of learning for the young fawn. The doe increases the fawn's range of travel. She leads it to new sources of food and water. When the doe munches leaves or fruit, the fawn watches. Then it does what she does."

Tim watched the band of deer wander out of sight. He hoped Blackie's mother would teach him well and keep him safe.

Chapter

What's for Dinner?

Tim saw a band of deer! Four does stood right in the thicket. "Gramp, the thicket looks prickly and brown. How do deer eat that stuff?"

"They like it, Tim," Gramp explained. "They thrive on it. They especially like thatch palm berries. But there are over 150 native plants that they eat. Food is plentiful.

"And speaking of food, we need to go to the grocery store."

"Where is it?" asked Tim.

"It's in the small shopping mall right on the National Key Deer Refuge," answered Gramp.

Gramp drove slowly along Key Deer Boulevard. Along the way, they saw a car parked beside the road. A man, a woman, and three children got out of the car.

Traffic around them came to a stop. Everyone looked where they were looking.

"What's going on?" Tim strained against his seatbelt for a better view.

Gramp said, "Someone's spotted a deer. Probably a tourist. We can't blame them for being interested. But . . ."

Tim pointed out his window. "Look, Gramp! I see the deer. The woman's trying to take its picture.

"Oh! And look at the kids. One of them has marshmallows. Another one has a bag of chips. They're coaxing the deer closer so their mom can snap a picture."

Gramp pulled the car to the side of the road. He said, "It's against the law to feed the deer. Human snack food isn't good for them. Too much of it endangers their health. And there's another danger too."

"What's that, Gramp?" Tim asked.

Gramp explained, "Feeding the deer along the roadway coaxes them to danger. They come looking for handouts. Each year many deer are hit and killed by cars."

Gramp picked up a booklet from the seat. It was from the refuge. He got out of the car and handed it to the family. Gramp told them just what he had told Tim.

Gramp returned to the car. He drove on to the grocery store.

Now Tim had more things to worry about. Would well-meaning tourists feed Blackie snacks? Would marshmallows and chips make him sick? What if people coaxed Blackie to the road? What if a car hit him?

Chapter

The Buck Stops Here

Gramp bought milk and bread at the grocery store. Then he and Tim drove along the back roads on the island. At one place, Gramp stopped the car and pointed. "Look, Tim. What do you see?"

Tim peered into the thicket for a moment. He saw nothing except leaves and branches. Then, at last, he saw a slight movement. "Deer, Gramp. Two of them."

"You have sharp eyes, Tim. Yes, two male deer. Two bucks. You don't see them much this time of the year."

"Why is that?" Tim stared at the bucks
as Gramp drove on.

"The bucks stay in the thickets. They
seem to keep to themselves. They don't
care for the fawns the way the females
do," Gramp explained. "Remember the
band we saw in the thicket? All females.

"We see more bucks in the fall. That is
when they are looking for mates."

"Why do some have bigger antlers, Gramp?" Tim asked.

"The antlers change as the buck grows," Gramp said. "You can estimate a buck's age by his antlers.

"A buck with simple antler spikes is usually one year old. If he has two tines on each antler, he's probably two. After that, antler growth slows down."

"What if he has four tines on each antler?" Tim asked. "I'd like to see one like that."

"He'd probably be four or five years old," Gramp answered. "Or he could be as old as nine. But the size of the rack doesn't mean he's the strongest. His strength is in his neck and shoulders.

"Each year in February and March, the bucks shed their racks. Without their antlers, the bucks all look about the same."

"Do the antlers grow back?" Tim asked.

"Oh, yes. The antlers grow back. But it takes a few months for them to sprout and grow. By the end of summer, the racks have grown back."

Tim laughed. "Mother Nature must have planned it that way. I'm glad the bucks are without antlers now while

Blackie's a fawn. I won't have to worry about them hurting the fawn or its mother."

"Tim, there's an interesting event happening tonight. You've become so good at spotting deer. Maybe you'd like to come along with me this evening."

"What will you be doing?" Tim asked.

"I'll let it be a surprise. Think you can wait?"

Tim loved surprises. But he could hardly wait until that night.

Chapter 7

Let's Count the Deer

That evening, Tim and Gramp drove to the Key Deer Refuge. The one-story white building looked gray in the twilight.

They joined a group of people in an office. They listened to the refuge manager.

"Tonight's our annual deer count," the man said. "You've done this before. You know what to do as you travel your special routes. So let's get started."

Once outside, Gramp joined a tall
blonde lady near a pickup truck. She wore
jeans and a T-shirt. And she carried a
notebook and a pen.

"Tim, this is Mary Vogel, a volunteer. I
drive the truck and help Mary count each
deer we see. It's a big job and an
important one."

"I'm pleased to meet you, Mary." Tim
shook her hand. "This is exciting! The
truck has spotlights! And you have a
flashlight! Do you use those lights to find
the deer?"

"Right, Tim," Mary said. "And you're going to help us count."

She gave Tim a notebook and pen. She showed him how to tally the count.

"We'll compare our counts at the end of the evening," Mary said.

Gramp laid a map on the dash. Then he started the truck.

"Each counter has a special area, Tim," Gramp said. "Two-thirds of the deer live on Big Pine Key. We'll stay right here on our own island.

"When we catch the deer in a bright light, they stand still," he explained. "They're easy to count."

Tim watched the truck's speedometer. Gramp was driving about 15 miles per hour.

He slowed down when they saw movement in a thicket. "There are five of them." He pointed in the deer's direction.

Mary and Tim both marked down the tally as they drove on.

"How many deer do you think live here?" Tim asked.

"Today, the herd is estimated at 600," Gramp replied. "About 40 years ago, people estimated the count at no more than 30."

Tim spotted several deer on the roadside. "Gramp! Mary! Why are some of the deer wearing collars?" he asked.

Mary explained, "Refuge workers have captured many of the deer. They have marked them with reflective collars. This helps scientists keep track of deer movement around the islands. When we see unmarked fawns, we assume they are new to the herd."

"Gramp, how do you know that you've counted every deer? They move about so quickly. And sometimes they hide. You might miss some. And you might count some twice."

"All deer counts are just estimates, Tim. But they show whether the herd is increasing or decreasing."

Tim's eyelids were growing heavy when suddenly he saw Blackie. "There, Gramp. To your left. See that black mark on his nose?"

"I believe you're right, Tim. It certainly looks like the fawn we saw in our yard."

Tim explained to Mary how Gramp saved Blackie from the collie. "I'm glad to know Blackie's still safe," he said.

By the end of the evening, they had spotted over 40 deer. Tim hoped the other groups had done as well. It was late that night before he and Gramp returned home.

Tim yawned, sleepy but happy. Counting deer had been like going on a treasure hunt. And seeing Blackie again was the best treasure of all.

Chapter 8

What's That Noise?

Summer turned into fall. Tim still caught glimpses of Blackie now and then. His fawn was surviving.

One day, Tim thought he saw a buck attacking a palm tree. It butted its head against the tree trunk. It rubbed its antlers against the palm branches.

"Gramp! What's going on? What's that deer doing?"

"He's trying to rub the velvet from his antlers," Gramp said. "While a buck's antlers grow, a protective skin covers

them. We call the skin *velvet*. The skin
falls off when the antlers are full-grown."

"This bothers the buck because sometimes it hangs in his eyes like rags. It makes him wild. So he tries to rub it off and clean his antlers. Once his antlers are clean, the buck feels strong again."

The next day, Gramp and Tim headed for the post office. They heard a great crashing in the thicket. Two bucks were lunging at each other. Gramp pulled the car off the road so they could watch.

"What's going on?" Tim asked.

"It's September, Tim. The beginning of the mating season. The bucks are *in rut*. They are ready to find mates. And sometimes that involves fighting to win the females."

Tim watched the bucks circle each other. They snorted. They pawed the ground. Then they walked toward each other cautiously. They lowered their heads and each gave a big push. The shoving match began.

The two bucks fought for position. All the while, they tried to hold their ground. Every now and then, the crash of the racks could be heard.

"Wow!" Tim exclaimed. "They could kill themselves."

"Right," Gramp agreed. "And sometimes they do. The rutting season is wild in the deer kingdom."

"The deer often hurt each other. They chase each other into traffic. They chase the females. There are many accidental deaths during this season."

Tim felt relieved when the bucks stopped fighting. One buck ran off in defeat. The other chased after a doe that had been standing nearby.

"Now what?" Tim asked.

"When the doe is ready to come together with the buck, she'll stop running. She'll allow him to approach her, and she'll accept his attentions. They will mate."

"For a lifetime?" asked Tim.

"No," Gramp said. "Just for a day or two. Then the buck will be off chasing another doe. That's nature's way of keeping the species alive. Next spring, you may see another fawn in my yard."

Tim wasn't interested in next year's fawn. He just wanted to see Blackie again. What if one of those bucks chased Blackie?

Chapter

Humans and Deer Living Together

Now and then, Tim did catch sight of Blackie. He had a small knob on each side of his head. He wouldn't have spikes until the following summer when he was one. He had survived.

Now Blackie was older and stronger. Tim knew Blackie could protect himself against the many dangers on Big Pine Key.

"Gramp," Tim said, "I'm glad that people on Big Pine want to protect the deer."

"The deer are cute," Gramp replied. "And they are unique. They're conversation pieces. They are something to tell your friends back home about."

"I think there's another reason people protect the deer," Tim said. "People don't want to see this species disappear, become extinct."

"You're right," Gramp said. "Lots of people want to protect the deer. But some people don't like the deer at all."

"Why not?" Tim thought of Blackie. He couldn't imagine anyone not wanting to protect Blackie.

"Those who dislike the deer have many reasons." Gramp looked into the distance. "Sometimes the deer destroy their gardens. They eat the leaves from their trees and plants. They even get into compost piles."

"So why don't people fence their yards?" asked Tim.

"Strict building codes prevent that,"
Gramp answered. "Scientists feel the deer
need to roam free in order to get the food
they need."

"Who else dislikes the deer?" Tim
asked.

"People in a hurry. Some people dislike the slow speed limits on Big Pine Key."

"Who else?" Tim insisted.

"Land developers," Gramp replied. "Current laws make it hard for people to get building permits. That means they can't build houses or places of business.

"Land developers would like to see Big Pine Key grow. They would like to attract more tourists. Tourists are big business. They spend lots of money."

"So who will win?" Tim asked. "I vote for the deer. But I suppose there are two sides to every question."

"That's right, Tim. Right now, there are many arguments over the deer. But today, refuge workers ask visitors to do just three things. Enjoy the deer. Take only memories. Leave only footprints."

Tim smiled. "That works for me."

Tim hated to see his stay with Gramp come to an end. But school had already started in Iowa. He missed his mother. And he needed to get home.

He had enjoyed Blackie and all the other deer. He was taking lots of memories with him. And behind him, he saw his footprints blending with Gramp's. It had been a great visit. He knew he would never forget Blackie and Big Pine Key.

Chapter

Key Deer Facts

Key Deer: (*Odocoileus virginianus clavium*) a subspecies of the Virginia white-tailed deer

Height   between 24 and 28 inches

Weight   does: 45–65 pounds
bucks: 55–75 pounds
fawns: 2–4 pounds at birth. Their hoofprint is the size of a thumbnail.

Color   fawns: tawny gray/brown. Their spots disappear with age.
adults: gray/brown. The underside of their tails are white.

Features   Bucks have racks of antlers. The antlers are usually simple spikes for one-year-olds and two tines for two-year-olds. Antler growth slows after the deer's second year.

Family Life   Does and fawns form a family band. They travel together for life. An older doe leads the band, which consists of her fawns and their fawns.
The bucks keep to themselves. They mate with many does during their rutting season from September to December.

Habitat   Big Pine Key, Florida, and a few surrounding keys. The Key deer are found no other place in the world. The National Key Deer Refuge covers about 7,000 acres of land in this area.

Food   red, black, and white mangrove trees; thatch palm berries; and over 150 other species of plants. Key deer can tolerate small amounts of salt in their water. But freshwater is essential for their survival.

Enemies   Large dogs, cats, and raccoons can attack and kill tiny Key deer fawns. Human predators are always a danger, although laws prohibit deer hunting.

Friends	Pulitzer prize-winning artist J. N. "Ding" Darling brought national attention to the plight of the Key deer in a 1934 cartoon. It showed tiny deer fleeing big dogs and gun-toting poachers. Ordinary people, both adults and children, wrote to their congressmen pleading for the deer. Because of those pleas, The Boone and Crockett Club in New York City and the National Wildlife Federation gave money to hire a warden to patrol the Key deer habitat. Jack Watson, refuge manager during the 1960s and 1970s, made protecting the Key deer his chief project.
Population	In the 1940s, it was estimated that only 30–40 Key deer existed. Today, refuge workers along with researchers from Texas A&M University estimate the size of the herd at 600. The refuge manager says, "The deer population boom proves that our programs to preserve the Key deer have been successful."
Dangers	traffic. U.S. Highway 1 runs through the deer refuge. Road kill is the number one cause of deer deaths. Canals that have been dug to allow residents access to their boats can be death traps for the deer. During the wild rutting season, bucks sometimes chase does into the canals, where they drown. Well-meaning tourists coax the deer to their cars in order to snap a picture or to give them a snack. This activity harms the deer's healthy diet and draws them into traffic.